FORCES OF NATURE

Tornadoes

By S.L. Hamilton

Visit us at
www.abdopublishing.com

Published by ABDO Publishing Company, PO Box 398166, Minneapolis, MN 55439. Copyright ©2012 by Abdo Consulting Group, Inc. International copyrights reserved in all countries. No part of this book may be reproduced in any form without written permission from the publisher. A&D Xtreme™ is a trademark and logo of ABDO Publishing Company.

Printed in the United States of America, North Mankato, Minnesota.
102011
012012

 PRINTED ON RECYCLED PAPER

Editor: John Hamilton
Graphic Design: Sue Hamilton
Cover Design: John Hamilton
Cover Photo: Getty
Interior Photos: AP-pgs 12-13, 15 (inset), 16-17 & 24-25-Waterspout-The Florida Times-Union/Jason Pratt; Corbis-pgs 4-5, 14-15, 21 & 28-29; FEMA/Greg Henshall-pgs 18-19; Getty Images-pgs 1, 9, 10, 11, 13 (inset), 20-21, 23, 26-27 & 32; National Oceanic and Atmospheric Administration-pgs 7, 8, 9 (inset), 11 (top), 16 (all insets) & 22; Photo Researchers-pg 6 (inset); Thinkstock-pgs 2-3 & 30-31.

ABDO Booklinks
Web sites about Forces of Nature are featured on our Book Links pages. These links are routinely monitored and updated to provide the most current information available.
Web site: www.abdopublishing.com

Library of Congress Cataloging-in-Publication Data

Hamilton, Sue L., 1959-
Tornadoes / S.L. Hamilton.
       p. cm. -- (Forces of nature)
Includes index.
ISBN 978-1-61783-262-8
1. Tornadoes--Juvenile literature. I. Title.
QC955.2.H36 2012
551.55'3--dc23
                              2011029674

Contents

Twister!

A tornado is a column of air that spins at destructively high speeds. It can be a few yards in width or wider than one mile (1.6 km). Any size tornado turns the air around us into a powerful and violent force of nature.

XTREME FACT – *The United States has more tornadoes than any other place in the world. In an average year, more than 1,000 tornadoes whirl destruction across the lower 48 states.*

A tornado threatens a house near Mulvane, Kansas, in June 2004.

The Science

Tornadoes develop from intense thunderstorms known as supercells. During these storms, warm, moist air near the ground moves in an updraft to clash with fast-moving cool, dry air in the upper atmosphere. With the warm and cold air currents blowing in different directions, a spinning column takes shape and hits the ground as a tornado.

A supercell thunderstorm in Oklahoma.

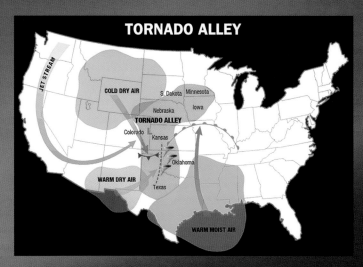

TORNADO ALLEY

JET STREAM

COLD DRY AIR

S. Dakota   Minnesota

Nebraska   Iowa

TORNADO ALLEY

Colorado   Kansas

Oklahoma

WARM DRY AIR

Texas

WARM MOIST AIR

Tornado Alley (in pink) is a name for the area in the U.S. where a great number of tornadoes form each year. The peak tornado season is usually May and June, but tornadoes can form at any time of year.

Classifications

The National Weather Service classifies tornadoes:
    Weak (under 110 mph/177 kph)
    Strong (110 to 205 mph/177 to 330 kph)
    Violent (over 205 mph/330 kph).
The Fujita scale classifies tornadoes based on the amount of damage done to the areas they hit. F0 is minor damage, while F5 is incredible devastation.

*A weak tornado
begins to dissipate.*

XTREME FACT – Only 2 percent of tornadoes are "violent," but they cause about 70 percent of all tornado deaths.

FUJITA SCALE DAMAGE EXAMPLES

F1-Moderate   **F2**-Considerable **F3**-Severe   **F4**-Devastating **F5**-Incredible

Since the Fujita scale is based on damage, not how big the funnel cloud is, it is possible for a large tornado to be weak and a small tornado to be incredibly violent.

An F4 tornado strikes the town of Pampa, Texas, on June 8, 1995.

Historic Tornadoes

Destructive, killer tornadoes have swept the Earth for thousands of years. Some will always be remembered.

The March 1925 Tri-State Tornado ripped an incredible 219-mile (352-km) path of destruction. Beginning in Missouri, it blasted through Illinois, and finally ended in Indiana. The deadliest tornado in history, it killed 695 people.

Survivors sit in the rubble of their home in hard-hit Murphysboro, Illinois.

On May 27, 1896, an F4 tornado ripped through St. Louis, Missouri, moved across the Mississippi River, and hit East St. Louis, Illinois. It became the third deadliest and most costly tornado in history.

Tornado damage in St. Louis, Missouri, 1896.

An F5 tornado struck downtown Waco, Texas, on May 11, 1953. Without warning, 114 people died, and hundreds were injured by the surprise tornado. One of the worst tornadoes in Texas history, it led to the development of a severe warning system.

People of Waco, Texas, scramble to find survivors in the rubble left by the 1953 tornado.

Infamous Tornadoes

The strongest and greatest numbers of tornadoes occur in the nation's midsection in spring and early summer. They usually form between the hours of 4-9:00 pm. However, if conditions are right, a tornado may hit anywhere and at any time.

A 1.5-mile (2.4-km) -wide tornado hits Tuscaloosa, Alabama, in April 2011.

 XTREME FACT – *Tornadoes kill about 60 people each year. The deaths are mostly from flying or falling debris.*

Tuscaloosa-2011

From April 25 to April 28, 2011, a vast supercell thunderstorm spurred the development of more than 300 tornadoes that struck areas of the central and southeast United States. Tuscaloosa, Alabama, was utterly devastated by one of these large tornadoes on April 27, 2011.

Joplin-2011

XTREME FACT – Some people believe that a tornado's low pressure causes buildings to "explode." In fact, it is high winds and flying debris that cause most damage.

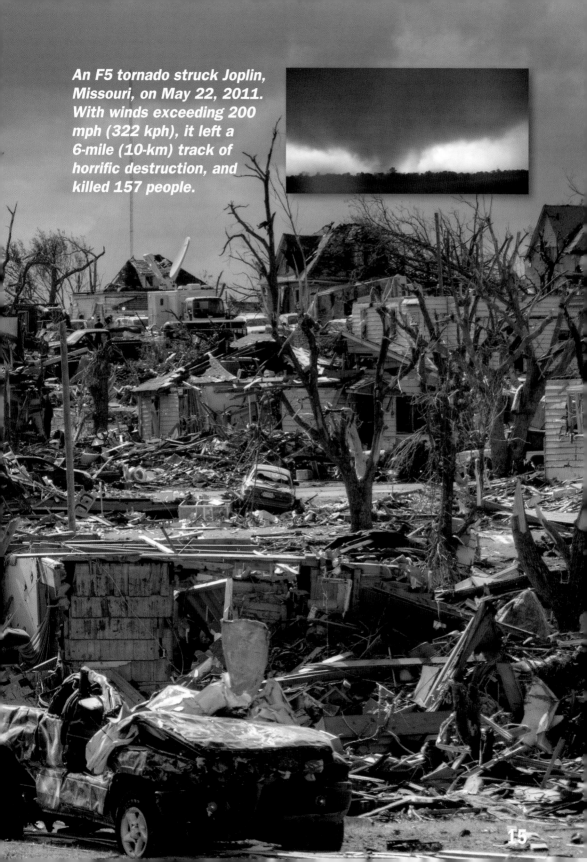

An F5 tornado struck Joplin, Missouri, on May 22, 2011. With winds exceeding 200 mph (322 kph), it left a 6-mile (10-km) track of horrific destruction, and killed 157 people.

Super Tuesday-2008

Super Tuesday is the day presidential primary elections are held in many states. On February 5, 2008, a warm evening spawned at least 84 tornadoes across 9 southern states, which swirled into the morning of the next day. One of the largest February outbreaks, the tornadoes caused 57 deaths.

Super Tuesday tornadoes caused deaths in Arkansas, Tennessee, Kentucky, and Alabama.

Mobile homes are not safe during a tornado. People should be prepared to move to a shelter.

Super Tuesday tornadoes caused $400 million in damages.

A funnel cloud touches down in Atkins, Arkansas, at about 5:00 pm on Tuesday, February 5, 2008. Due to the tornado outbreak, Super Tuesday voting was shut down early in some areas of Arkansas, Missouri, Illinois, Alabama, and Tennessee.

XTREME FACT – 81 percent of deaths on Super Tuesday happened because many people did not have access to a basement or other protected shelter.

Greensburg-2007

Greensburg, Kansas, 12 days after the tornado struck in 2007.

The first F5 tornado of the 21st century blasted through the town of Greensburg, Kansas, on May 4, 2007. With wind speeds of 205 miles per hour (330 kph), 95 percent of the town was destroyed.

XTREME FACT – The Greensburg tornado's winds were so powerful that some of the 11 people who died were killed while sheltered in their basements.

Veterans Day-2002

Rare November tornadoes struck on November 9, 2002. Widespread storms spawned 76 powerful tornadoes that blasted through 17 states, from Indiana and Ohio to Alabama and Mississippi. The tornadoes finally dissipated on Veterans Day, November 11. It was the second-largest November tornado outbreak in history, with 36 people killed.

With winds of 207-260 mph (333-418 kph) a tornado turned an Ohio factory to rubble and tossed a semi trailer onto its side during the November 2002 Veterans Day outbreak.

An F4 tornado destroyed a movie theater and tossed cars into the seats in Van Wert, Ohio, in 2002.

Oklahoma & Kansas-1999

Winds wrapped a pickup truck around a tree.

Supercell thunderstorms created 74 tornadoes that swept across Oklahoma and Kansas on May 3, 1999. Near Oklahoma City, an F5 tornado spun for 90 minutes, moving along a 38-mile (61-km) path. It killed 42 people, and caused $1 billion in damages.

A tornado touches down south of Anadarko, Oklahoma, on May 3, 1999.

XTREME FACT – A tornado once destroyed a motel in Oklahoma. The motel's sign was later found in Arkansas, 30 miles (48 km) away!

The tornado's path of destruction through an Oklahoma City suburb.

Waterspouts

A waterspout is a tornado that forms over warm water. Air and mist swirl at gale-force speeds– 60-120 mph (97-193 kph). The height of a tornadic waterspout may be from 300-2,000 feet (91-610 m).

A waterspout moves across the St. Johns River in Jacksonville, Florida, in June 2009.

Storm Chasers

Storm chasers photograph and prepare to deploy scientific equipment in front of an F4 tornado in South Dakota in 2003.

Storm chasers put their lives on the line to videotape, photograph, and deploy scientific equipment in front of oncoming tornadoes. The objective is to learn as much as possible about these deadly forces of nature. This knowledge may lead to early warning systems that help save lives.

XTREME FACT – So far, no storm chasers have been killed by tornadoes. However, several have been hit by lightning or been killed in traffic accidents while escaping tornadoes.

Surviving a Tornado

If tornado warnings are broadcast, immediately take shelter in a basement or other underground refuge. Bring a radio or other device and listen to updates. If there is no basement, move to an interior area with no windows, like a bathroom or closet. If in a car, try to get to a shelter. If that's not possible, leave the car and get as low as you can. Cover your head.

Sylvia Hess gestures to the rubble-covered basement where she survived a direct strike by an F5 tornado in Greensburg, Kansas, in 2007.

Glossary

CATASTROPHIC
Great danger that is often sudden or unexpected, which typically leads to great losses of life and property.

EARLY WARNING SYSTEM
A system put into place that uses weather radar and local storm spotters to collect information and issue early warnings to people when conditions are right for hazardous, life-threatening weather, such as tornadoes.

FUJITA SCALE
A scale created in 1971 by Dr. Tetsuya Fujita and Allen Pearson for measuring the amount of damage a tornado causes to buildings and plants in a specific area. It ranges from F0 (the least amount of damage) up to F5 (incredibly destructive and violent).

FUNNEL CLOUD
A rotating column of air that is not in contact with the ground. Once a funnel cloud touches ground, it is called

LOW PRESSURE
An area where the atmosphere's pressure is lowest as compared to the surrounding area. Low pressure areas are usually accompanied by rain clouds, rising air, and winds flowing counterclockwise. These conditions may lead to the creation of funnel clouds and tornados.

NATIONAL WEATHER SERVICE
A United States government agency that provides weather forecasts and warnings.

SUPERCELL
A thunderstorm with a constantly rotating updraft of air that often creates a tornado.

TORNADO ALLEY
A nickname for an area that consistently experiences a high number of tornadoes year after year. These states include parts of Minnesota, South Dakota, Iowa, Nebraska, Colorado, Kansas, Oklahoma, and Texas. These Great Plains states are relatively flat, which allows the cold, dry polar air from Canada to meet with warm, moist tropical air from the Gulf of Mexico. When these two air masses collide, conditions are right for tornadoes to form.

Index

One of the closest photographs ever taken of a tornado.